Raptor World

Eagles

by Jenna Lee Gleisner

Bullfrog Books

Ideas for Parents and Teachers

Bullfrog Books let children practice reading informational text at the earliest reading levels. Repetition, familiar words, and photo labels support early readers.

Before Reading

- Discuss the cover photo. What does it tell them?
- Look at the picture glossary together. Read and discuss the words.

Read the Book

- "Walk" through the book and look at the photos. Let the child ask questions. Point out the photo labels.
- Read the book to the child, or have him or her read independently.

After Reading

- Prompt the child to think more. Ask: Eagles are very strong. They can hunt and carry prey larger than themselves. Can you think of other animals that hunt animals larger than themselves?

Bullfrog Books are published by Jump!
5357 Penn Avenue South
Minneapolis, MN 55419
www.jumplibrary.com

Library of Congress Cataloging-in-Publication Data

Names: Gleisner, Jenna Lee, author.
Title: Eagles / by Jenna Lee Gleisner.
Description: Bullfrog books edition.
Minneapolis, MN : Jump!, Inc., [2020]
Series: Raptor World
Audience: Age 5-8. | Audience: K to Grade 3.
Includes index.
Identifiers: LCCN 2018038131 (print)
LCCN 2018039066 (ebook)
ISBN 9781641286275 (e-book)
SBN 9781641286268 (hardcover : alk. paper)
ISBN 9781641288200 (pbk.)
Subjects: LCSH: Bald eagle—Juvenile literature.
Classification: LCC QL696.F32 (ebook)
LCC QL696.F32 G59 2020 (print)
DDC 598.9/43—dc23
LC record available at https://lccn.loc.gov/2018038131

Editor: Susanne Bushman
Designer: Jenna Casura

Photo Credits: Michal Ninger/Shutterstock, cover; Eric Isselee/Shutterstock, 1; KatPaws/iStock, 3; Montreal _ Photos/iStock, 4, 23tl; Heinz Hudelist/imageBROKER/SuperStock, 5, 23br; Aurora Photos/SuperStock, 6–7, 23bl; FloridaStock/Shutterstock, 8, 10–11, 23tr; KenCanning/iStock, 9; IdealPhoto30/iStock, 11; Javier Fernández Sánchez/Getty, 12–13; Stefan Huwiler/imageBROKER/SuperStock, 14; KaidoKarner/iStock, 15; Paolo-manzi/Shutterstock, 16–17; Richard Seeley/Shutterstock, 18–19; JamesBrey/iStock, 20–21; Serjio74/iStock, 22; AlecOwenEvans/iStock, 24.

Printed in the United States of America at Corporate Graphics in North Mankato, Minnesota.

Table of Contents

Fast Divers

This is a bald eagle.
See its white head?

This eagle is brown.
It has gold specks.
It is a golden eagle.

Eagles soar.

They see well.

This eagle spots a fish.

Where?

One mile (1.6 kilometers) away!

It dives.

How fast?

Up to 100 miles (161 km) per hour.

Cool!

prey

Eagles have sharp talons.

Why?

To catch prey!

The golden eagle dives faster.

How much faster?

Twice as fast!

Wow!

Two hunt together.
One chases a fox.

The fox gets tired.

The other eagle grabs it.

They eat.
With what?
Sharp beaks!
Yum!

beak

They will fight.

Why?

To get food!

Wow!

What will they eat next?

Built to Hunt

wings
Eagle wings are large, long, and strong. They help eagles soar. The average wingspan is 7 feet (2.1 meters). They flap hard and help eagles carry heavy prey.

feathers
Layers of feathers keep eagles warm. Bald eagles have white head and tail feathers.

beak
Eagle beaks are hooked. This helps them tear and eat food. Bald eagle beaks are large and yellow. Golden eagle beaks are smaller and gray.

talons
Sharp talons help eagles grab, carry, and hold onto their prey.

Picture Glossary

bald
Having little or no hair. Bald eagles have white feathers on their heads, so they appear bald from a distance.

prey
Animals that are hunted by other animals for food.

soar
To fly or glide high in the air.

specks
Small spots or marks. Golden eagles have gold specks on their brown feathers.

Index

To Learn More

Finding more information is as easy as 1, 2, 3.

1. Go to www.factsurfer.com
2. Enter "eagles" into the search box.
3. Click the "Surf" button to see a list of websites.